COSTUMES FOR COLORING

Fashions
Then & Now

Illustrated by Roberta Collier-Morales
Text by Kate Braungart and Sarah Gross

Grosset & Dunlap • New York

Color your way through fashion history! FASHIONS THEN & NOW spotlights a whole range of spectacular styles, from the trailing gowns and steeple hats of medieval times, through the huge hoop skirts of the Civil War era, right up to today's hot designer clothes.

Each picture in this book is a snapshot of a particular moment in the fashion time line, starting back in the 1100s. The clear, accurately detailed drawings are printed back-to-back with fun facts on what everyone was dying to wear...and why. This way, a finished page can be removed with the informative notes still attached!

This unique book offers the double pleasure of creative coloring and exploring the fascinating world of fashion.

Coronets

Kings, queens, and princesses were not the only ones who wore crowns in the Middle Ages. Some stylish headdresses, called *fillets* or *coronets*, looked like crowns and were worn by many fashionable women. Also popular during the twelfth century were long, trailing sleeves that were tight at the shoulder and wide at the elbow. Sometimes sleeves were so long that they dragged on the floor, and women had to tie the ends in big knots so they wouldn't trip over them!

Two-in-One

From 1350 on, the most fashionable dress for women was actually *two* dresses—a tight-fitting underdress called a *kirtle*, and a looser overdress called a *surcoat*. The look was completed with a low-slung belt (worn under the surcoat!) and a favorite medieval headdress, the *hennin*. Hennins were cone-shaped with a silken veil trailing behind. Fashion demanded that not a single strand of hair be visible, so women tucked their long locks up inside their hennins and painfully plucked the hair from their necks and foreheads.

Slashing

In the early 1500s, Germany was first in fashion. *Slashing*, in which clothing was cut and the cloth lining underneath pulled through, was one German style copied throughout Europe. At first just sleeves were slashed, as on these women's dresses, but as the style became more and more popular, clothes were slashed from top to bottom.

Elizabethan

Queen Elizabeth I, with her slender, straight figure, was a real fashion trendsetter during her reign (1558-1603). Wealthy women everywhere wanted to copy her look, but that was not easy. First they squeezed themselves into *corsets* (skinny vests that could be tied tightly), then they put on a hoop called a *farthingale* that made their skirts stand out, and finally they put on the gown, which usually had a stiff top that came to a deep point below the waist. But that wasn't all. Lace was invented during this era, and the queen favored a huge, wired lace collar. Elizabeth tried to put a stop to her copycats. She passed laws forbidding her subjects to wear lace and limiting the size of their collars!

Ruffs

Around 1550, *ruffs* became a huge fashion craze. They started as small decorations at the neck, but gradually they grew larger and larger until people looked as if they had giant lace wheels on their shoulders. Some ruffs stood out as much as twelve inches from the neck! These enormous ruffs were so popular that silversmiths had to make long-handled spoons just so people could feed themselves!

Fontange

In the 1690s, a new type of headdress caught on. It was the *fontange* (sometimes called the *tower*), a pleated, starched, wired lace frill that stood up straight from the top of a woman's head. Although the fontange first appeared in the court of the French king Louis XIV, he hated the new fashion so much that he forbade women to wear it. They didn't listen to him. Legend has it that in 1714, an English duchess showed up at court without one and was personally complimented by the king. After that, the fontange lost its popularity.

Wigs and Panniers

High style for eighteenth-century noblewomen meant elaborate powdered wigs and wide, wide gowns covered with ribbons, lace, frills, and bows. *Panniers*, circular metal frames flattened toward back and front, were what gave gowns their great width. Panniers became all the rage, following the motto "the bigger, the better." Wigs also were quite huge; some towered three feet above a lady's head. These wigs were often more trouble than they were worth. Ladies couldn't get through doors, and sometimes their wigs even caught fire on the ceiling chandeliers!

Colonial Lady

Europe set the fashion trends during the 1700s, and American women eagerly awaited word of the latest styles, though news of what was "in" took months to travel across the Atlantic. One style that colonial women picked up from their English counterparts was the low-crowned, wide-brimmed straw hat. For years, straw hats had been worn by country people because they were cheap and easy to make, but during the eighteenth century they became stylish for fashionable ladies as well. Many of them wore their new straw hats over a little lace cap and tied under the chin with a wide, colored ribbon.

Greek Revival

The French Revolution touched off a true revolution in clothing. Before, huge panniers, richly decorated gowns, and ridiculously high powdered wigs were the styles set by the king and queen of France. (The extravagance of their rulers was one of the things that sparked the people's rebellion.) After the Revolution, fashion turned to a new simplicity, inspired by the clothing of ancient Greece. Dresses were filmy and narrow, with high waists and short sleeves. Heels were out and simple sandals laced with ribbons were the in-thing. Even the style of women's hair—with little curls along the forehead and in the back—was copied from centuries-old Greek statues and sculptures.

Ruffled Hems

By 1815, dresses were still high-waisted, but they were no longer simple. The most noticeable difference was the hemline. First, skirts were shorter so that a woman's ankles showed, and second, the hems were elaborately decorated with ruffles, puffs, lace, or embroidery. Puckered, puffed, or bunched sleeves were also popular. For outside strolls, women always wore bonnets, often trimmed with flowers or ruffles to match their hems.

Coats and Capes

Fashionable outerwear in the early 1800s was often as pretty as the dress it covered. Capes and coats came in a mix of styles—short or long, and plain or trimmed with fur, braid, or fancy embroidery. Fur muffs also were popular, even though ladies almost always wore gloves.

Gigot Sleeves

By the 1830s, high waists were out and tiny waists were in. With the help of a corset, a woman could make her waist look smaller by lacing herself tightly before putting on her dress. This was not only painful, it sometimes resulted in broken ribs! Skirts, worn over layers of petticoats, were growing wider. But perhaps the most distinctive style of the 1830s was the huge *gigot* sleeve. Women had discovered that a small waist looked smaller if not only the skirt was large, but the sleeves were, too, and so sleeves grew and grew until they reached almost ridiculous sizes.

Crinolines

The beautiful dresses of the late 1850s hid a brand-new invention, a steel-framed petticoat called the *crinoline*. Weighing only a half-pound, the crinoline replaced the six or seven heavy petticoats that had been needed to give a gown fashionable fullness. This meant a woman could move around much more freely, and dance more easily as well. But wearing a crinoline took practice. It could sway and tip up, showing more of a lady's ankle than was thought proper. And sitting down gracefully was a challenge.

Bloomers

A woman wearing pants is commonplace today, but back in the 1850s the idea was thought absurd. A style of baggy pants called *bloomers* was named after the woman who tried to make them fashionable almost 150 years ago. Mrs. Amelia Bloomer—an American—was tired of all the frills and fuss in fashion and wanted more comfortable clothing. At first, everyone laughed at her for being so radical, but after the bicycle was invented in the 1870s, bloomers made perfect sense. Women no longer had to ride bikes wearing heavy, long skirts. Little girls especially were happy with the new style, since it made playtime less of a hassle.

Bustles

In the 1870s, a fashionable ball gown had to have a *bustle*—a cage-like support that held up the skirt in the back—and a train. This elaborate gown was made by a dressmaker, and only the wealthiest women could afford it. But when a man named Isaac Singer invented the first practical sewing machine in 1851, fashion was changed forever. Clothes could now be made faster and in greater quantities. Ready-made clothes began popping up in the stores at reasonable prices. Days of hand-sewing entire dresses were slowly fading, as people dropped their sewing needles and picked up their purses to buy these new, more affordable fashions.

Day Dress

This slightly shorter-length dress from the 1880s was perfect for strolling about town or through the park. The bodice had rows of buttons down the front and a high-necked collar, and different mix-and-match patterns were common neighbors on one dress. Women often wore hats topped with fluffy ostrich feathers, and a new haircut called the *fringe* was popular. Today we call the style *bangs*.

Leg-of-Mutton Sleeves

Puffed sleeves grew bigger and bigger, and by the late 1890s they became known as *leg-of-mutton* sleeves. This funny name was used because the sleeves actually resembled a leg of lamb, a popular dish at the time. To shield themselves from the sun on afternoon strolls, ladies carried frilly umbrellas called *parasols,* and wore wide-brimmed hats (which often looked like upside-down bowls) decorated with flowers or feathers.

Gibson Girl

This style of dress is named for a popular artist of the early 1900s, Charles Dana Gibson. In his magazine sketches, he drew fashionable young ladies with a certain posture called the *S-bend*. A new shape of corset made this stance possible. Many women admired these attractive magazine models in their swirling skirts and imitated the *Gibson girl* style.

Straight Silhouettes

World War I started in 1914 and had a great effect on fashion. With so many men away fighting, women took on new activities to help out with the war effort. Because they needed to move around easily, skirt lengths shortened, showing ankles and legs for the first time in nearly a century. Even after the war had ended, people were less formal in their dress. Dresses were straight and fairly simple, and a woman could get away with not wearing a hat in public.

Flappers

The trendsetters of the 1920s were the *flappers*—young women giddy with the end of World War I and their newly won right to vote—who loved to have a good time. Instead of the corseted, stately look of their mothers and grandmothers, flappers took on a free, boyish style. Skirts were shortened, waists dropped to the hips or disappeared altogether, and dresses were beaded, feathered, and fringed. Flappers smoked, danced wild new dances like the Charleston, and, perhaps most shocking of all, cut their hair short. It was a revolution in style.

Fur-Collar Coat

Wearing fur in the 1920s and '30s was considered the ultimate in glamour. The designer Coco Chanel created the narrow fur-trimmed coat with its face-framing collar, and it appeared in endless variations. Fake pearls were being factory-made, which meant that women could afford to wear long, long strands draped around their necks. The *cloche* hat, a snug cap which fit over the ears, was made in wool, silk, and velvet, and sometimes even gold or silver lamé, to sparkle during fancy evening parties. Film, a recent invention, popularized the fashions of the day and became an important tool for advertising current styles. Young women followed these trends, wanting to look as graceful and sophisticated as their favorite film stars.

Hollywood Chic

Hollywood had become the official capital of filmmaking by the 1930s, and movie stars like sophisticated Joan Crawford and dancing duo Fred Astaire and Ginger Rogers paved the way for fashion much as royalty did hundreds of years before. Different stars touched off different trends. The soft, flowery gowns worn by some movie heroines were adopted by their audience, while the screen siren in slinky satin was the model for other fans.

Military Style

In the 1940s everything was rationed for World War II, including fabrics. The War Production Board said that buttons for decoration, turned-back cuffs, and flaps on pockets all were wartime no-no's. Hemlines went up to save material, and rich, luxurious fabrics were not used very much. Penny-pinching was a national pasttime, and people wanted long-lasting, durable clothing. The war also influenced styles. Small hats were worn cocked to the side, with military-style suits like this one.

The New Look

By the 1950s, when World War II was over, everyone was sick and tired of rationed fabrics and practical clothes. They wanted luxury and glamour—which is just what they got. The designer Christian Dior created the "New Look," made up of a very full skirt with a form-fitting top. This style became very popular, very fast. It was an affluent era, which allowed for the huge amount of fabric needed to make the skirt. Twenty-five yards of material could be used for one dress alone! To give skirts the fullness designers wanted, crinolines and petticoats were worn underneath.

Minis and Go-Go Boots

After the formal '50s (when housewives on TV were shown wearing dresses, pearls, and heels while cleaning the floor), the 1960s brought a totally different style. Minidresses with colorful geometric patterns turned up on the fashion scene. A British model called Twiggy popularized the very skinny, boyish figure. Girls wore high boots with their miniskirts. Designers also created futuristic clothes made of linked metal disks or shiny metallic fabrics—sometimes even clear plastic!

Hippies

Love beads, bell-bottoms, and a new attitude of freedom took over in the 1960s and '70s. The United States was involved in the Vietnam war, and many people objected to the war and the military draft. They wanted peace and a feeling of brotherhood among all countries. Rock and pop concerts, held in fields or parks, were major hangouts for hippies and flower children, and at these events a new style was obvious—psychedelic patterns, layers of flowing fabrics, and exotic clothing from countries such as India and Afghanistan. For a while, the tie-dye fad had people personalizing their own clothes with swirls and splotches of bright color.

Swinging Seventies

During the 1970s, trendy nightclubs called discotheques—discos for short—sprung up all through the United States and Europe. It was a whole new party scene and disco-goers started wearing clothes which were fun and great for dancing. While flashing lights played over the darkened floor, the dancers spun and twirled in exotic eveningwear, including glittery jewelry, sequins, rhinestones, high strapped heels, leotards, wraparound skirts, and soft, swirly dresses.

Power Suit

In the 1980s, more women than ever before headed into the business world. They began to share responsibility, important titles, and power with men. For climbing the career ladder, women needed professional outfits that were businesslike but also feminine. Major fashion designers noticed this need, and voilà! The power suit was born.

Late Night

Evening wear in the 1980s included a wide range of styles of dress, but short and strapless were definitely "in." Colors like teal green and seashell pink, combined with glossy fabrics, sequins, or taffeta, made these dresses perfect for high school proms or fancy parties. Hair might be done in a French braid or pulled back and spritzed with hair spray, and pumps or heels were often dyed to match the dress.

Long and Short

The motto for the '90s seems to be "anything goes." Skirts can be floor-length, mini, or anywhere in between. This design manages to be two lengths at once! Modern designers often combine styles of the past and transform them into something new.

Runway Glamour

One of the most popular styles of the '90s is the *slip dress*. Simple ones are worn casually, often with a T-shirt underneath, while slip dresses in silk and satin show up at formal functions. Here is a glamorous designer version, along with a two-piece evening gown by Valentino, which allows just a glimpse of midriff.